P9-EKR-417

In this glossary:

[a] is pronounced as in far
[e] is pronounced as in get
[ee] is pronounced as in feet
[i] is pronounced as in sit
[o] is pronounced as between got and goat
[oo] is pronounced as in loose
[y] is pronounced as in yes

[kh] is pronounced as in Scottish loch
[zh] is pronounced as in vision

CALGARY PUBLIC LIBRARY

JUN   2011

Other books available from Ethnic Enterprises

Ukrainian Folk Tales Retold in English:

7. Carrots to Coins
6. Oil in the Borsch
5. The Worry Imps
4. Boris Threeson
3. How April Went to Visit March
2. Zhabka
1. The Raspberry Hut

Humorous stories of the old days:

Vuiko Yurko Second-Hand Stories
Vuiko Yurko The First Generation

Baba the Cook

I Can't Find the Words to Tell You

Kharkiv

Dream Star Stories

From the Gallows
The Lost Testimony of Louis Riel

A Cottage for Kip

Feet on the Pillow

and Other Ukrainian Folk Tales Retold in English

Retold by Danny Evanishen
Translations by J Zurowsky
Illustrations by Ralph Critchlow

Published by
Ethnic Enterprises
Publishing Division
Summerland, BC
Copyright © 2001

Copyright © 2001
Daniel W Evanishen

All rights reserved. The use of any part of this publication
reproduced, transmitted in any form by any means, electronic,
mechanical, photocopying, recording, or otherwise, or stored in
any retrieval system, without the prior written consent of the
publisher is an infringement of the copyright law.

Canadian Cataloguing in Publication Data

Evanishen, Danny, 1945-
Feet on the pillow and other Ukrainian folk tales retold in English

ISBN 0-9681596-5-6

1. Tales--Ukraine. I. Zurowsky, J., 1954- II. Title. GR203.8.E9323
2001   398.2'09477   C00-911389-4

Ethnic Enterprises
Publishing Division
Box 234
Summerland, BC
V0H 1Z0
http://www.ethnic.bc.ca

Printed and Bound in Canada
by New Horizon Printers, Summerland, BC

1 2 3 4 5 6 7 8 9 10•10 09 08 07 06 05 04 03 02 2001

Table of Contents

Dedicated to the children.

Foreword

This book is the eighth volume in this series. There will be more books as long as I have the stories to fill them. That should not be a problem; the Ukrainian culture is very rich in this way, and there are thousands of tales.

I enjoy collecting and publishing these stories, but they are sometimes hard to find. Many people know the stories, but for various reasons, don't get around to writing them down or recording them.

In this day and age, writing down the stories is becoming more and more important, as the people who know the stories either die or forget the stories. It is up to us, now, to save this very important part of our heritage.

As in the first seven volumes of the series, some of the tales to be found in this book are old favorites, while others are less familiar.

If anyone has tales they would like to contribute, please send them to me at:

Danny Evanishen
Box 234
Summerland, BC
V0H 1Z0
devanishen@img.net

Acknowledgments

In this book, some of the translations from Ukrainian were done by my father, John W Evanishen and some by J Zurowsky. Natalka Evanishen, my mother, provided my very first folk tales and always had lots of encouragement for me. Ralph Critchlow did the illustrations.

Thanks are always due to the libraries and archives across Canada which make their material available. A list of all the stories and their sources will eventually be published.

The photograph on the back cover was taken by Mich Cheladyn.

This book contains versions of stories submitted by the following: Sandra Fedoruk (*Feet on the Pillow, Gossip, Over the Fence*), Mary Shewchuk (*The Devil at the Wedding, The Sheep and the Fox*), Rena Patrick (*The Falcon Hunter and the King, The Wonderful Plant*) Myrtle Anderson (*Gossip*) and Robert Larionyk (*Garlic*).

Thank you to everyone who sent their stories to me, thinking I would find them interesting. I definitely find them interesting.

— Danny Evanishen, Publisher

Cossack Mamaryha

Cossack Mamaryha worked for rich people for twenty-five years and earned three copper coins. He collected his pay and then went on the road wherever his eyes would lead him. As he went along the road he met a lad.

"Good day, young fellow," he said.

"A good day to you," was the reply. "And who are you?"

"I am Cossack Mamaryha. I served rich people for twenty-five years, earned three copper coins and went into the world following my eyes. And who might you be?"

"I," said the lad, "was hired by a lord to harvest his rye and found in the field a hair bag that gives me food and drink by itself. But the lord found out about this bag and ordered that I be beaten and the bag taken away. I just took my bag and fled."

"May I see this bag?"

"Robbers in the forest attacked and took it away from me."

"Well, let us travel together. You shall be like a brother to me."

They walked on and met a second lad.

"Good day, lad," they said.

"And a good day to you too," he said. "Who are you?"

"I am Cossack Mamaryha and this is my blood brother. Who are you?"

The lad replied, "I served a lord. While chopping wood in the forest, I found a wire bag on a tree, a bag that does any type of work for you. But the lord found out about the bag and ordered me beaten and the bag taken. But I did not wait for him. I took my bag and fled."

"And where is the bag?"

"Robbers in the forest took it from me."

"Come travel with us, then. You will be a brother to us."

They walked and walked and met a third young fellow.

"Good day, lad!"

"And a good day to you, gentlemen. And who may you be?"

"I am Cossack Mamaryha and these are my blood brothers. And who are you?"

"I served a lord. When I took the horses to pasture, I found in the meadow a pair of boots with which you can walk over the water. But the lord found out about them and wanted to beat me and take the boots. So I ran away."

"Where are these boots?"

"Robbers in the forest attacked me and took them away."

"Come with us and you shall be a brother to all of us."

The four went on together. Sometimes they begged for bread and sometimes they worked for food; then they moved on. They came to a crossroads where four roads ran off four ways.

Cossack Mamaryha stopped and said: "Here, brothers, we must split up. I have three copper coins. Each of you take one and choose a road. Follow the chosen road, and I will take the road that is left."

He gave each a copper coin. They said farewell and went their separate ways, each on a different road. Cossack Mamaryha went on by

14

himself; he wandered for three years. One day while walking along a great forest he came to a wide clearing where he saw four men fighting. He said to them, "Good day, good people. What are you fighting for?"

They replied, "We have a hair bag that gives food and drink by itself, a wire bag which does any type of work by itself, boots with which you can walk on water and the horse named Hever. We are fighting over how to divide these goods, as we all want them."

"Aha!" thought Cossack Mamaryha. "These are the robbers I have heard about." Aloud, he said, "Let us see if I cannot help you. Are you agreed to listen to me, Cossack Mamaryha? No one will settle things among you better than I."

"Agreed," said the robbers. "Divide the goods among us, Cossack Mamaryha!"

He said, "Place on the ground beside me the hair bag, the wire bag, the boots and the horse Hever and you all go to the far end of the clearing. When I wave my hand, all of you run toward me together. Who gets here first will select that which he likes the most; then the second will select, and the third, and the fourth will take what is left."

The four robbers went to the end of the clearing and Cossack Mamaryha wasted no time. Immediately, he threw the bags onto his back, put on the boots and jumped onto the horse.

"Hey, Cossack," said the horse, "how am I to run, over the trees or over the ants?"

"Over the trees!" said Cossack Mamaryha.

When the horse flew over the trees, the robbers saw, and they ran back, but how were they to catch the horse Hever?

Cossack Mamaryha rode far on the horse and thought, "I must find my blood brothers and return their wealth which was taken from them by those robbers. I will give them back their bags and the boots, while the horse Hever shall remain with me." And he began to look throughout the wide world for them.

In a long time or a short time, he arrived at a large house. As he asked for water to drink, the master came out of the house and asked, "Who are you, and where are you going?"

"I am Cossack Mamaryha," he said, "and I go in search of my blood brothers."

The man hugged Cossack Mamaryha. "I am your blood brother who once found a hair bag and ran away from a lord," he said.

"I have brought you back your hair bag," said Cossack Mamaryha.

The blood brother led him to the house, placed him at the table and gave him a feast. Cossack Mamaryha gave the hair bag to him.

"No," said the brother, "I will not take the bag. Let it be yours. Your copper coin brought me fortune and happiness. I have become rich and live in plenty. I do not need the bag."

Cossack Mamaryha stayed with his blood brother for three days, then said farewell and rode off in search of the other two.

In a long time or a short time, he arrived at a still richer manor. The master came out; it was the second blood brother who found the wire bag and fled from the lord. He met Cossack Mamaryha with honor and declined the offer of the wire bag.

He said, "I became rich from your copper coin and now live well. Let the bag be yours."

Cossack Mamaryha visited with him for three days and then left to search for the third brother. He rode and rode over the wide world and came to a rich mansion, richer than the other two. The master came out; it was the third blood brother. He hosted Cossack Mamaryha with respect, but refused the boots.

"From your copper coin," he said, "I have all I need, and have no use for the boots. Why must I walk on the water? But they may be useful to you."

After three days, Cossack Mamaryha said farewell to his blood brother and rode further into the world to wander, seeking his fate and fortune. He rode and rode until he was tired and then stopped by the road and got out the wire bag. He said, "Wire bag, set up a tent!"

Immediately, out of the bag came servants, and they instantly set up a tent and then returned to the bag.

Cossack Mamaryha then untied the hair bag and said, "Hair bag, I am hungry!"

Instantly a table appeared, laden with various food and drink. When he had eaten his fill, he said, "Bag, clean up!"

All was cleaned up and back in the bag as it was before.

Cossack Mamaryha wandered thus for a long time, and eventually he came to a foreign land. There he heard from the people that in front of the palace of their king stood a mighty oak tree with a countless fortune buried in its roots. The king had announced that whoever cut down the oak, pulled out the roots and got the fortune for him would receive half his kingdom and his daughter as a bride. So far, nobody was able to even cut down the tree.

Cossack Mamaryha heard, and he said, "Let us try to cut it down!"

He rode to the palace and said that he had come to chop down the oak. The king asked, "Who are you?"

"I am Cossack Mamaryha," he said. "I can get the treasure from under the oak for you."

"Well," the king said, "if you can chop down the oak and get the treasure, then I will sign over to you half of my kingdom, and give you my daughter, the princess, as a bride. But if you do not do this in one night, then your head will come off your neck."

Cossack Mamaryha went to the oak and opened his bag, saying, "Wire bag, chop down the oak, pull out the roots and get the treasure!"

Out of the bag came servants who went to work. Cossack Mamaryha lay down and rested. It was not yet midnight when the oak was chopped down, the roots were pulled out and the treasure was brought up.

The king could not sleep. He arose before dawn, went to the oak and was struck dumb. There was no oak! Where it had stood was a deep hole, and by the hole were large chests and in them, gold and diamonds, an immeasurable treasure.

Cossack Mamaryha awakened. "See," he said to the king, "it was all done last night."

"Truly it has been done," said the king. "Now you may have my daughter."

But the princess protested; she did not want to marry Cossack Mamaryha.

"Why should I marry a simple Cossack?" she asked.

"There is nothing to be done," said the king. "You must go."

They had a wedding celebration and the king signed over half his kingdom to Cossack Mamaryha. But Cossack Mamaryha said, "What is half a kingdom to me? Your kingdom is small. Sign over all of it to me."

"If you do not want it, that is your decision," said the king, "but I will not give you all of it."

Cossack Mamaryha brought out his horse Hever and took his wife by the hand. He said to the king, "If you will not give me the kingdom, then I shall travel with my wife to another land."

He mounted his horse and sat his wife before him.

"How shall we ride?" asked the horse.

"Over the tops of the trees!"

The horse Hever carried them, and a large cloud of dust was raised. He carried them one day, then a second, down to the Black Sea. They flew over the sea where was no land, just waves passing by. At a rock in the sea, they stopped to rest. Cossack Mamaryha took the hair bag off his back and said, "Hair bag, give us food and drink."

A table appeared with food and drink such as the princess had never seen at her palace. They ate and drank their fill.

"Hair bag, clean up."

All was instantly cleaned up. Then they lay on the rock to rest. Cossack Mamaryha fell asleep while his wife quietly arose, took both bags and went to the horse Hever. She put her foot into the stirrup and the horse immediately asked, "Where shall I carry you?"

"Carry me to my father," she said.

The horse carried her and they were gone.

Cossack Mamaryha, after sleeping well, awoke and saw no horse, no wife, no hair bag and no wire bag. Only the boots lay beside him.

"Eh," he said, "if the boots are here, then Cossack Mamaryha will not perish!"

He put on the boots and walked on the water. He walked and walked two days until he had crossed the sea, and then he walked further. He spied a bush with red berries and, as he was hungry, Cossack Mamaryha picked one berry and threw it into his mouth; instantly a great horn grew on his head. He picked another berry and threw it into his mouth, and another large horn grew beside the other.

"Hey hey," he said, "how am I to live with these horns?"

Then he saw another bush nearby, on which bush the berries were also plentiful.

"Shall I try these berries?" he asked. "It cannot be any worse than it is."

He picked a berry from that bush and ate it and one horn fell off. He picked another berry, ate it and the other horn fell off. Then he picked berries from both bushes and went to the kingdom where his wife lived.

He changed his clothes and his appearance so that they would not recognize him and went to the palace.

In the courtyard he yelled, "Berries! Who will buy my berries?"

The princess heard and sent her servant girl. "Go," she said, "and see what kind of berries they are. Here they are only blooming, but somewhere they have already ripened."

The servant girl went down and asked, "Are the berries good or are they expensive?"

"They are both expensive and good."

"How much?"

"A silver piece for each berry."

The servant girl reported this to the princess and the princess gave her fifty silver pieces. She said, "Buy me those berries."

Cossack Mamaryha took the money, gave the berries to the servant and went on his way. The princess took two berries and threw them into her mouth; instantly, two giant horns grew on top of her head. The princess threw herself to the mirror and screamed. The king ran in and was terrified.

"What is this? What did you do?"

"I only ate two berries," the princess said.

"This cannot be," said the king. "How can two berries do this? Where are these berries?"

He threw some berries into his mouth, and instantly horns grew! The king was afraid, and then he became angry and ordered that they capture that man who sold the berries. The soldiers ran and searched but found no one. What to do now? How could the king and princess live with such horns?

The king summoned doctors and herbalists to drive away the horns. They gathered from the whole kingdom; they looked and looked but could do nothing.

The king sent messengers to other kingdoms, declaring that whoever could drive off the horns would receive the entire kingdom. Doctors came from foreign lands, but no matter how they thought, no matter with what they anointed, they could do nothing.

The princess cried, the king was enraged and the nation mocked and protested. "Why do we have a king with horns?" they asked. "We do not want such a king!"

Cossack Mamaryha came to see the king.

"Good day, father-in-law," he said. "Maybe I can help you."

"Oh, son-in-law, please help," said the king. "I will sign my whole kingdom over to you, just to be rid of these horns."

"Good," said Cossack Mamaryha, and he gave the king two berries from the other bush. As soon as the king swallowed them, the horns fell off. The princess pleaded, "My dear husband, give me some."

"No," he said. "I will not give them to you. What did you do with my horse Hever?"

"Your horse lives in the barn. Have mercy on me, give me a berry!"

"And the two bags — where are they?"

"Your bags are whole. They are in the bedroom hanging on a nail. Please save me!"

"Are you going to leave me again?"

"Never in eternity!"

Cossack Mamaryha threw a berry into her mouth and instantly a horn fell off. He threw in a second, and the other horn fell off.

"Now take care that you know how to honor a marriage," said Cossack Mamaryha.

Then they celebrated and drank mead and wine. The king signed over the kingdom to Cossack Mamaryha and they all lived happily together. The hair bag gave them food and drink and the wire bag did all the work, and the people enjoyed their lives.

The Devil at the Wedding

Once there was a rich family who lived at the edge of the village, in a large home with a large yard. One of the children was getting married, and they were having a wedding party to which the whole village was invited.

The Devil heard about the wedding, and decided that he would go, too. Maybe he would be able to join in the feast.

As the Devil started down the long driveway to the house, he spied a bush with a large pot hanging on a branch. The pot was used by the rich man to take oats to his pony.

The Devil hid in the bush under the pot, thinking that it would be a good place from which to get a good view of the wedding. From there, he would sneak in and join the party.

Several young boys happened along at that time. They also wanted to join the wedding. As they came up the driveway, one of the boys saw the pot hanging on the branch.

"I bet you cannot hit that pot with a rock," he said to the other boys.

At that, all the boys gathered up stones and began pelting the pot. What a delightful noise it made when they hit it!

The Devil could not stand the noise, so he ran out the other side of the bush. As he approached the house, he saw a big empty rain barrel by the back door.

"This will be the perfect place to hide," he thought, and he climbed in. "I will be right next to the kitchen, and I can steal some food when no one is looking."

The Devil peeked through the bung hole in the barrel, and found that he had a good view of the kitchen and part of the yard. He did not see the young boys come into the yard, but the boys certainly saw the barrel.

The boys picked up some sticks and poked them into the barrel, nearly blinding the Devil. Then they began beating the barrel to see if they could break it.

After beating the barrel with big sticks for a while, the boys went on, laughing. The poor old Devil had had enough. He fell out of the barrel and staggered away. His head was spinning and his ears were cracking from the beating the barrel had taken.

"I may as well go home," said the Devil. "If there are a dozen young boys at a wedding, the Devil is not needed there."

The Devil Serpent

Long ago and far away, there lived an old man and an old woman who did not have any children, although they wanted them.

The man went to the market, traded his goods for what they needed, bought some salt fish and drove home. As he was travelling, he became very thirsty from nibbling on the salt fish. Stopping at a well, he leaned over to get a drink. Suddenly a devil in the water grabbed his beard and hung on tight.

"Let go!" yelled the man.

"No, I will not," answered the devil.

"Why do you not want to let go?"

"Give me what is the most valuable to you, and then I will let you go," said the devil.

The man said, "What is the most valuable? I have horses at home, take them."

"No," said the devil and held on tighter.

"I have oxen," said the man, "take them."

"No," said the devil.

The man named everything he could think of and the devil refused everything. The man became desperate and said, "I have an old wife at home; take her, but let me go."

"No," answered the devil.

The man thought, "If he will not take my wife who I left to the end, and she is the most valuable of all, then what am I to do? I can think of nothing else but to agree to what he says."

"Take what you think is the most valuable, then," he said to the devil.

They signed a document to that effect, and the devil released him.

The man got on his wagon and drove on.

While he was away, his wife had given birth to two children, who grew not by the day nor by the hour, but by the minute. By the time the man got home, they were already beautiful children and still growing.

As soon as the wife saw her husband, she ran to meet him with the children. The man saw the children and almost fainted. Then he told her of his adventure.

"My dear wife! I was riding from the market and needed a drink of water. I bent over a well and a devil in the water grabbed my beard and did not let go. I pleaded and begged him, but he would not let go. 'Give me what is the most valuable at home, then I will release you,' he said. I offered him the oxen and the horses, but he did not take them. 'I have a dear wife,' I said. 'Take her, but just let me go.' But he did not.

"He insisted I give him what is most valuable to me. Since we had no children when I left home, I did not consider them. But now, where will we hide them so as not to give them up?"

"Yes," said the wife, "we must hide them somehow. We will dig a hole under the house, at the back wall, and hide them there."

They dug a hole beneath the back wall, put food and water in the hole, and hid the children there. They covered the top, painted it over and then left the house.

Shortly after, the devil in the form of a serpent came to the house. He looked about the house and saw no one there.

He found the poker by the pich and asked it, "Poker, where has master hidden the children?"

The poker said, "My master is good to me. He stokes the fire with me and treats me well."

Not receiving an answer from the poker, the devil asked the broom, "Broom, where has your master hidden the children?"

The broom said, "My master is a good man. He sweeps the pich with me and treats me well."

The devil then asked the ax, "Ax, where has your master hidden the children?"

The ax said, "My master is a good man. He chops firewood with me and treats me well."

The devil then turned to the chisel and said, "Chisel, where has master hidden the children?"

The chisel said, "My master is a good man. He uses me to punch holes and treats me well."

But the devil serpent said to him, "Is your master really such a good man? Look how he has beaten your head."

"That is true," said the chisel. "Carry me to the back wall of the house and throw me over your shoulder. Where I fall, you must dig there."

The serpent did this and where the chisel landed, he dug. Soon he had dug out the children and carried them off.

Becoming tired, the devil serpent sat down to rest, and he fell asleep. The girl cried beside his head, while the boy sat and worried. Then a horse ran up to them and said, "Greetings, young friends. Are you wandering by your own free will or through enslavement?"

The boy replied, "Oh, Brother Horse, not of our own free will, but through enslavement."

"Climb onto my back," said the horse. "I will take you away from here."

They got on the horse while the serpent slept, and the horse jumped up and ran. When the serpent awoke and saw that the children were not there, he came after them, flames shooting from his mouth.

The boy said, "Oh, Brother Horse! I feel the breath of the devil serpent; my back is burning. We shall all be destroyed."

The serpent chased them, breathing fire. The tail of the horse began to burn. The horse saw that he could not escape, so he threw the children off his back. He ran off while the serpent caught the children. He said to them, "Why do you try to escape me? I shall eat you!"

The brother and sister pleaded for him not to eat them. The serpent then said, "This time I will forgive you, but from now on, do not listen to anyone but me!"

The serpent carried them until he became tired and sat down to rest and again fell asleep. The girl cried beside his head while the boy sat and worried. And then a bee flew by. He said, "Greetings, young friends! Are you wandering by your own free will or through enslavement?"

The boy replied, "Oh, Brother Bee, not of our own free will, but through enslavement."

The bee said, "Climb onto my back. I will take you away."

"How can a bee carry us when the horse could not?" asked the boy.

"Whether I do or not," said the bee, "it is all the same, as you shall perish by the hand of the devil serpent."

They climbed onto the bee and he carried them away. The serpent, when he awoke, saw that they were gone and gave chase. After a time, the lad said, "Oh, Brother Bee, my back is burning. We shall all perish."

The bee, seeing that he could not escape, turned his wings over and dropped the children. They fell down while he flew away. The serpent rushed in and opened his jaws wide.

"Now you have fallen into it!" he said. "Now I shall eat you. I told you not to listen to anyone but me."

They pleaded with the serpent, and he relented a second time. He again carried them off. Once more, he grew tired and fell asleep. The girl cried beside his head and the boy sat and worried. Along came a scrawny ox who said, "Greetings young friends! Do you wander of your own free will or through enslavement?"

"Oh, Brother Ox, of our own free will we would not have wandered here. We are trapped by the devil serpent."

"Climb on my back," said the ox. "I shall carry you away."

"But the horse and the bee could not free us; how can you do it?"

"It is nothing," said the ox. "Climb on and I will carry you away."

They climbed on and the ox carried them away. The ox ran so fast that each minute was a mile, and if you blinked, then it was two. The serpent, when he saw that they were not there, became very angry and ran after them, roaring and spewing fire.

The boy turned around and said, "Oh, Brother Ox! My back is beginning to burn. We shall all perish!"

The ox said, "Look in my left ear; pull out a comb and wave it behind you."

The lad found the comb and waved it. Instantly the forest behind them became as thick as a comb. The ox ran and ran, each minute a mile, and if you blinked, then it was two.

The serpent, when he came to the forest, began to chew his way through it. He gnawed through all the trees and ran after them. The boy turned and saw that the serpent was gaining on them and said, "Oh, Brother Ox, my back is burning. We shall all perish."

But the ox said, "Look in my right ear, pull out a little kerchief and wave it before me."

The lad pulled out the little kerchief and a sea appeared before them, with a golden bridge over it. They ran onto the bridge and crossed to the other side. The boy waved the kerchief behind, and the bridge vanished. The serpent ran to the sea and stopped, for he could not cross the sea.

The ox said, "I shall carry you to a little house and in this house you will live not far from the sea. But you must kill me."

The brother and the sister cried, "How can we kill you when you saved us from death?"

"It is nothing," he said. "Kill me and cut me in four pieces. Hang one quarter over the hearth, the second quarter in the corner by the pich, the third in the corner with the icon, and the fourth near the doorway."

They did as the ox commanded and hung his four quarters up as instructed, then lay down to sleep. The brother awoke in the night and saw near the doorway a horse in beautiful finery.

He looked in the corner with the icon, and there was a magic sword which could chop by itself. On the floor in the corner was the hound named Proteus while on the hearth was the hound named Nedvyha. When the sister awoke, the lad took the sword, mounted the horse and, with the hounds, went hunting.

They lived by the sea, the brother hunting and the sister taking care of the house. One day while the brother was hunting, the serpent cast a spell on the girl. He then called to her, "How did you cross the sea?"

The enchanted girl replied, "My brother has a little kerchief that makes a bridge appear when he waves it."

The serpent commanded her, "Tell him you want to wash the kerchief. Then wave it and I will cross over and live with you and we will get rid of your brother."

That evening she said to her brother, "Give me the dirty kerchief, brother. I will wash it."

The brother believed his sister and gave her the kerchief. Next day, the sister went to the sea and waved it, and the golden bridge appeared. The serpent crossed the bridge and said to the girl, "When your brother comes home, act sick and say you dreamed that if he went hunting and got you some milk from a wolf, then you would be cured. He will go hunting, and the wolves will tear his hounds apart. Then we will be able to take care of him, because his strength is in those hounds."

The brother returned home from hunting. The serpent hid while the girl said, "I am very ill. I dreamed, brother, that if you got me some milk from a wolf and I drank it, maybe I would be cured, because I am so weak!"

"I shall get the milk for you," said the brother. He rode to the forest, where a wolf appeared. Proteus caught her, and Nedvyha held her. The brother milked her and let her go. The she-wolf turned about and said, "Thank you for releasing me. I feared that you were going to kill me. In gratitude, I will give you this wolf cub."

She said to the young wolf, "Serve this man as you would your own father."

The sister and the serpent saw the brother coming with the two hounds and the wolf. The serpent said, "It is bad that he obtained a third guard. Pretend to be more sick and beg of him some milk from a bear. The bears will tear him apart without a doubt."

The serpent changed himself into a needle, which she stuck into the wall. The brother came to the house while the hounds and the wolf tried to get into the house and attack the needle.

The sister said, "Why do you keep those dogs? They do not give me any peace!"

The brother yelled, and the hounds sat down. The sister said, "I dreamed, brother, that if you got me some milk from a bear, I would drink it and be cured."

"I shall get it," he said. In the morning he rode off to find milk from a bear. Approaching the forest, he spied a she-bear which appeared out of nowhere. Proteus caught her and Nedvyha held her. The brother milked her and released her. The she-bear said, "Thank you, lad, for releasing me.

For that, I will give you a bear cub." She said to the cub, "Obey him as your own father."

The brother rode home and the sister and the serpent saw that there were now four behind him. The serpent said, "Ask him for some milk from a fox, and when he rides off, then the animals shall eat him."

He transformed himself into a needle, and she stuck him higher into the wall, so that the hounds could not reach him. The brother came to the house and the hounds threw themselves into the house towards the needle. The sister began to cry, "Must you keep so many hounds?"

The brother yelled, and the hounds sat down. The sister again began her story, "I dreamed brother, that if you got me some milk from a fox, then I would be cured."

"I shall get it," said the brother.

He lay down to sleep, Nedvyha at his head, Proteus at his feet, and the wolf and bear at his sides. In the morning he got onto the horse and, with his animals, rode off.

Approaching the forest, he saw a fox appear. Proteus caught her and Nedvyha held her, while the brother milked her and released her. The fox said, "Thank you for releasing me. I thought that you were going to tear me apart with your hounds. For that I will give you a young fox." She said to the fox, "Obey this man like your own father."

The brother rode home. The serpent saw that he had acquired a fifth guard. He gnashed his teeth and said, "Become still more sick, and tell him you dreamed that in a distant kingdom is a wild boar who ploughs the land with his snout, sows grain with his ears and harrows with his tail. In this kingdom there is a mill on twelve stones that grinds by itself, pours grain by itself, and fills the sacks by itself. If you got flour from beneath all twelve stones, then you could bake yourself a flatcake and be cured."

When he heard this from his sister, he became angry and said, "You are not acting like a sister to me, but more like an enemy!"

She said to him, "How can I be an enemy to you when there are only the two of us here?"

The brother believed her again and rode off with his guards. He finally found the kingdom with the magic boar and the magic mill. There he saw twelve stones and twelve doors which opened and closed by themselves.

He took some flour from beneath the first stone and went to the second door, but the doors

closed quickly and the animals were trapped. When he had gone through all the doors, he went outside and saw that his animals were not there. He whistled, but only heard them howling somewhere. He could not find them, so he sorrowfully rode home.

When he got home and saw his sister dancing with the serpent, he knew that he had been tricked. As soon as he entered the house, the serpent said, "Now I have you, young man! You will make a fine meal for me!"

The snake ordered the brother to chop firewood and put water on the stove to boil, so that he could be cooked. As he chopped the wood, a magpie flew to the brother and said, "Take your time, young lad, take your time; your animals have chewed through two doors."

He filled the pots with water and began to heat them. But he had chopped rotten firewood and splashed water on it so that it would not burn. He went outside to chop more firewood.

The magpie said, "Take your time young lad, take your time, because your animals have gnawed through four doors."

When he took the wood into the house, the serpent said, "You cannot even boil water, you useless thing!" The serpent took the poker himself, pushed it into the stove, and the wood caught fire. But the brother spilled water on the wood and it burned slowly.

Again he went outside for wood and the magpie told him, "Take your time, young lad, take your time, because your animals have gnawed through ten doors."

The brother took the most rotten wet wood and threw it into the stove. Finally the water began to boil. Again he went outside for wood and the magpie told him, "Take your time, young lad, take your time, because the animals have gnawed through all the doors and are resting."

Finally, all the pots with water were boiling, and he said to the serpent, "Your Honor, please allow me to climb into a tree so that I may say goodbye to the wide world."

"Go ahead and climb," said the serpent.

The brother climbed the large ash tree, and did not miss a single branch; he stepped on each one to waste time. He climbed to the very top.

The magpie flew to him again and said, "Take your time, young lad, take your time, because your animals will soon be here."

The impatient serpent shouted, "How long will you sit there? Come down immediately!"

The brother began to climb down and again stepped on each branch. Just as he stepped on the last branch the animals ran in and stood around him. He jumped down and called to the serpent, "Come out now, Your Honor. I am ready!"

The serpent came out and the brother said to the animals, "Wolf! Bear! Proteus! Nedvyha! Grab the evil serpent!"

The animals charged and ripped the devil serpent to shreds.

The brother immediately burnt the corpse, and the fox swept the ashes with her tail, carried them into the field, and scattered them to the winds. But as the serpent was being ripped apart, the sister found one of his teeth and hid it.

The brother said, "Sister, if you are such a person who will dance with a devil serpent, you should stay here, while I will go to another land."

He hung a pail on the ash tree and said, "Sister, if you are going to cry for me, this pail will be full of tears. If you are going to cry for the serpent, it will be full of blood."

He got onto his horse, took his faithful friends and rode off. He came to a castle and was told that in their well was a three-headed dragon. When the people went for water, they sacrificed a young girl to the dragon; otherwise, they could get no water. That day it was the turn of the king to bring his daughter.

The lad said, "I can defeat this dragon."

"If you do," said the king, "I will give you my daughter as a bride and half my kingdom."

The king and the princess went to the well, and behind them came the young lad with his animals. The dragon came out to eat her, but the young lad said, "Sword, chop him up! Wolf, Bear, Proteus, Nedvyha, grab him!"

The self-chopping sword cut the dragon, while the animals tore him to pieces. They burned the corpse and the fox swept the ashes with her tail, carried them into the field, and scattered them to the winds. The people thanked the lad, and the princess gave him a ring.

They went toward the castle, but the lad was tired and he lay on the grass to rest, the princess near him. A lackey came to them, untied the self-chopping sword and said, "Self-chopping sword, chop him up!"

The sword chopped the lad into little pieces, but the animals had fallen asleep and did not hear

anything. The lackey said to the princess, "You will say that I saved you from death. If you do not, the same shall befall you as befell him."

The princess was afraid and agreed. They came home and the king was so happy that he ordered everyone to begin a celebration.

When Nedvyha awoke, he saw that his master was not there, and woke everyone up. They began to think what to do, and they decided that the fox should run to get some water of life and a young apple.

The fox ran off to get the water of life and the apple. She came to the well with the water of life and by it grew an apple tree guarded by a soldier. The soldier was strong and swung his sword so swiftly that not even a fly could come near the well.

The fox pretended to limp, and went by the well, where she stumbled. The soldier ran after her thinking that he would catch her. The fox led him far from the well, and then ran back to it. She filled a little bottle with water, picked an apple and ran off as fast as she could.

Proteus took the water of life and poured it onto the pieces of the young lad and they joined together. He poured some water into his mouth and the lad came alive. He gave him the young apple and the lad became stronger and more handsome than he was before. The young lad got to his feet and said, "Oh, I slept so long!"

"You would have slept forever if we had not had the water of life," said Proteus.

They decided that the lad should dress as a beggar and go to the castle, which he did. The guard would not allow him into the castle, but the princess heard him and ordered that the beggar be brought in. He entered the castle and took off his hat. As he did so, the ring that the princess gave him shone brightly. The princess saw the ring and said, "Come here, holy beggar. I shall treat you."

The princess poured him a goblet of wine and he took it with his left hand. She saw that he did not take it with his right hand, which had the ring, so she took the goblet back and drank the wine herself. She poured another, which he took with his right hand. She then recognized her own ring and said to her father, "This is my true husband. He led me away from death. And this one," she said, pointing to the lackey, "this evil person killed him and forced me to say that he was my husband."

The king became angry. He ordered a wild unbroken horse to be brought from the pasture. They tied the lackey to his tail and released him into the fields.

The young lad was welcomed to the table and they had a wedding party.

They lived happily together for some time. One day, the brother thought of his sister. He ordered his horse saddled and gathered his animals and rode to her. Arriving, he saw that the pail was full of blood. He knew that she still pined for the serpent and said, "Since you are still such a person, I do not want to know you any more. Stay here, and I shall never come to see you again."

She pleaded and begged and finally convinced him to take her with him.

When they arrived at the castle, she placed the tooth of the serpent under the pillow he slept on. The brother lay down to sleep and the tooth killed him. His wife thought that he was angry because he did not speak to her, and she pleaded with him not to be angry.

She then took his hand, but the hand was cold as ice. She screamed, and Proteus ran into the room. He looked at the dead lad, and kissed him. The tooth left the lad, who came alive, but killed

Proteus. Then Nedvyha kissed Proteus; Proteus came alive and Nedvyha died. Then Proteus said to the bear, "Kiss Nedvyha."

Nedvyha came alive but the bear died. Then the turn came to the fox. If she died, there would be no one left to kiss her. But the fox was smart; she put the bear on the doorstep and kissed him and quickly jumped behind the door. The tooth flew out of the bear, but missed the fox and got stuck in the door.

They burned the door and the tooth, and the fox swept the ashes with her tail, carried them into the field, and scattered them to the winds. At that moment, the spell was broken forever and the sister became her proper self again. She begged for forgiveness from her brother, which he willingly granted.

Then they had a big celebration and, from that day on, they all lived in peace.

The Falcon Hunter
and the King

Long long ago, a king lived in a castle, protected by his royal guard, who went everywhere with him. Often, when he was not needed at court, the king would look out the window at the far-away mountains, wondering and dreaming of what life must be like there.

It was not likely that he would ever find out, as he had been a king or a prince all his life, and was not allowed to wander about. Quite frankly, he was bored with his kingdom and everything that went with it.

One day a guard came to the king and said, "We have caught someone trespassing on the royal grounds, Sire. We have thrown him into the dungeon. What shall we do with him?"

"Send him to me," replied the king. "He can dine with me this evening."

The prisoner was surprised to be in the presence of the king, and he explained how he happened to be hunting, and followed his falcon onto the grounds without knowing it.

"I am sorry to be a bother to you, Your Majesty. If I had known I was on your grounds, I would not have trespassed. I am an honest hunter, and I respect the laws of whatever country I happen to be in."

The king was extremely interested in what the hunter was saying, and he pressed for more details of his free life of travel. The hunter told the king of many places he had been and of the strange sights he had seen.

"Tell me more," said the king. "Tell me also of the people you have met and the animals you have hunted."

The hunter was only too happy to find that he was not in serious trouble, and he talked and talked, while the fascinated king drank it all in. They talked all night, and finally had some sleep early in the morning.

When the hunter awoke, he was told that he was free, and he happily went on his way.

The king, however, was not having such a good time. He barely slept from the thoughts that passed through his mind. He would dearly love to see the places the hunter had spoken of, and he longed to have the same adventures and meet the same people.

After this, whenever he looked at the blue mountains, the king would add the stories he had heard from the hunter to his dreams of what must be there. It must have been fantastic!

One day, the hunter returned to the castle. He brought with him a gift for the king. The gift was a baby falcon he had found while hunting. The hunter was welcomed by the king, and he stayed there for some time, training not only the baby falcon, but the king as well.

Up to this time, the king had servants for everything, and he really did not know how to do anything for himself. The hunter taught the king how to work with the falcon, and also all the other things that a hunter must know.

After the hunter had gone, the restless king decided to leave his castle. He thought long and hard about it, and finally, one night, he crept over the wall with his falcon. He dropped onto the ground on the outside of the wall, and he was free!

The king ran into the woods, but he soon got tired, as he had never run more than two steps since he was a small boy. This was going to be more difficult than he thought. And it was difficult. With the hunter at his side, he had learned many things, but he had never had to put them into practice.

The king persevered though and, bit by bit, he became more adept at the life of a free hunter. He wandered toward the warmer countries, so he did not have to worry about the weather and he was able to concentrate on his hunting. He soon became very good at it, and the falcon grew to be like a brother to him.

Years later, the king stopped in a village. As he was resting there, the royal guard came through proclaiming that there was to be a festival the next day. There would be music and dancing and a large feast. Of course, the king decided to stay for the celebration.

At the celebration, the king was struck by one song the musicians and singers were performing. It was a song about a far-away country, and how, one summer, a falcon had flown away with their king.

Feet on the Pillow

In the old days, the rich landlords owned everything, and the poor peasants worked the land, earning barely enough to survive. Often, the starving peasants would go into the woods and gather firewood, mushrooms or acorns, knowing full well that the landlord could have them severely punished for theft.

Petro was a young man who had been caught many times by the landlord and his guards. The landlord finally decided that, since nothing would stop Petro from his behaviour, he must be put to death.

On the day of his hanging, a large crowd gathered in the yard of the landlord. Petro was well-known to all the villagers, and they were sorry that it had come to this.

Before the rope was put on him, the landlord asked if Petro had one last request.

"I do, Your Honor," said Petro. "I would like one last look at this beautiful world."

The request being granted, Petro stepped into the middle of the yard, while the people stood back to make room for him.

"What a beautiful sky this is," cried Petro. "What beautiful clouds and sun! Soon my young eyes shall see thee no more! No more will my ears hear the whisper of the breeze or the babbling of the brook!"

Petro carried on at some length, and the crowd became quite emotional. Some were openly weeping, and others stood looking at their feet.

Petro slowly made his way to the edge of the crowd, speaking all the while of how he would miss the world when he was gone.

Suddenly, he leaped the fence and was gone, as fast as his feet would carry him. At first, no one realized that he was gone and, by the time the guards came to their senses, it was too late. Petro was no longer there.

Petro ran for all he was worth, and finally came to his hut. He rushed in the door and flopped himself on his reed bed.

His surprised wife saw him come running, and when she followed him into the house, she saw him on the bed with his feet on the pillow and his head at the other end.

"What is happening?" she cried. "Are you crazy? Why are your feet on the pillow?"

Petro smiled and replied, "If it were not for my feet, this crazy head would not be on my neck. They saved my life, so they deserve the pillow, and they shall have it!"

72

Garlic

A long time ago, in a village in Ukraine, lived some people who were mostly farmers. They grew food for themselves and for their countrymen who lived in the towns and cities.

Usually, the people planted various crops, but one year, for some reason, they all planted garlic. The crop was extraordinarily good. The farmers had so much garlic that they could not eat it all or even sell it all to the people in the city.

A meeting was called to discuss the problem, and all the villagers gathered.

"We have too much garlic," said one of the farmers. "The townspeople have enough and will not buy any more, and we certainly cannot eat all that we have. What can we do with it before it spoils in the bins?"

The problem was discussed for some time and no solution appeared. There just happened to be a wandering storyteller in the village at that time, and he also attended the meeting.

"I was recently in a country to the east where I saw no garlic," he said. "Perhaps they would be interested in buying some."

"No garlic? Unbelievable!" said someone.

"Nevertheless, it is true," said the storyteller. "I do not know the reason for it, but they do not have any garlic."

"Then let us send our garlic to them," cried a farmer. "How can people live with no garlic?"

A committee was chosen, and they made plans to sell their garlic to the eastern country. Seven drivers with wagons were chosen, and the wagons were piled high with garlic and covered with skins to protect the garlic on the journey. The storyteller offered to go along to show the drivers the way, and they set off.

After some time travelling, the caravan of wagons reached the eastern country, and found that the situation was exactly as the storyteller had said. There was no garlic at all in the entire country. The farmers were pleased.

The eastern people were thrilled with the garlic. "This is wonderful!" they cried. "Why is it that we did not know of this wonderful food before? We must have this valuable garlic.

"We will buy this treasure from you," said the people. "In return, we will fill your wagons with what is most valuable in our country."

While the farmers wandered about and rested, the eastern people filled the wagons and covered them with the skins.

On the way home, the farmers discussed their successful trip. They were pleased with the way things had turned out.

"But this can only happen once," said one of the farmers. "They will surely plant the garlic and grow their own, and we will not be able to sell them any more."

"That is true," said the storyteller. "But did you notice that these people also did not have onions? I asked around, and they did not even know what I was talking about."

"Then we must plant onions next year," said one of the farmers, and they all agreed. They rushed home to tell their friends of their trip and of the plan to plant onions.

When the wagons arrived at their village, the skins were removed, and what should be in the wagons but gold! So that was the most valuable thing the eastern people had! This was good, and the farmers were more than pleased.

The following year, the onion crop was very good, and twelve wagons full of onions set off for the east. As they travelled, the farmers wondered among themselves how much gold they would receive this time.

"With twice as many wagons, we will surely get twice as much gold," they thought. "Then we can all hire workers to till our fields while we live like lords!"

At the eastern country, the farmers were once more successful in selling their crop.

"You have brought us another marvel," cried the eastern people. "You have made our lives happier. In return for the onions, we will fill your wagons with what we value most in our country."

The farmers rested while the wagons were being filled, but they did not see that the eastern country lacked anything else that they could produce. They would have to be happy with what they received, for the eastern people were sure to grow their own onions after the farmers had left.

The happy farmers dreamed of their life of leisure to come as they travelled, and they finally arrived at home. The entire village gathered to help unload the wagons.

"Once more we were successful," said the leader of the wagons. "The eastern people had never seen onions, and they were only too happy to buy them from us. In return, they filled our wagons with the most valuable thing in their country. Let us unload the wagons and share in the good life to come!"

The whole village ran to take the skins off the wagons, and were astounded to find every wagon filled with garlic!

Gossip

There was a young girl in the village who was a terrible liar and, even worse, a shameless gossip. She said many awful things about her neighbors and, even though people did not believe all of her lies, some of her bad words remained.

Since so many people in the village were being harmed by this behaviour, the people decided to ask for the help of the vorozhka.

Once things were explained, the vorozhka thought the matter over, and finally summoned the girl to come to her.

The girl was afraid of the powers of the vorozhka, but she could not refuse to come.

The vorozhka gave the girl a feather pillow. "Take this pillow to the top of the hill and shake the feathers into the wind," she ordered.

Relieved to have escaped so easily, the girl ran to the hill and scattered the feathers into the wind until there were none left in the pillow case. She then returned to report to the vorozhka.

"I have done as you asked," said the girl. "It was easy to do!"

"Good," said the vorozhka. "Now take the pillow case back to the hill and gather up every one of those feathers."

Of course, this was impossible to do, and the poor girl was reduced to tears as she chased around the fields trying to stuff the feathers back into the pillow case.

"So you see," said the vorozhka. "It is very easy to spread gossip, but next to impossible to repair the harm it does."

How Foolish Ivan
Married the Princess

There was a man who had three sons. Two were smart and the third was called Foolish Ivan. When the time came for the father to die, he called his sons and said that after his death, they were to go to the cemetery every day for three days.

The father died and was buried with respect, as was proper. The eldest son was to be the first to go to the grave, but he became sick. The middle son did not want to go in his place, so they called the youngest son, "You go to the graveyard, Foolish Ivan."

Foolish Ivan got down from the warm pich where he spent most of his time, got dressed, took a club into his hands and went to the cemetery. When he got there, he prayed and lay on the grave to rest. At midnight his father called from the grave, "Is that you, Stefan?"

"No, it is I, Ivan."

"Why did Stefan not come?"

"Stefan has become ill, Father."

"So be it," the father said. "Here is a knot of horsehair. If the need should arise, singe it with a fire and immediately a horse will appear. Climb into its left ear and out the right and there will be rich clothing for you. Just do not keep the horse for long. Once it has served you, let it go."

Saying this, the old man disappeared. Foolish Ivan slept well and went home.

"What did you see?" his brothers asked.

"What is to see in a graveyard at night?" said Foolish Ivan as he climbed onto the pich.

Next night, it was the turn of the second son. He did not want to go, as he was afraid. "Foolish Ivan," he said, "you go in my place."

"If you do not want to go, then I must," said Foolish Ivan. "I do not want Father to be angry."

"Father will not be angry," said the second son. "Just go."

Foolish Ivan went again to the cemetery and again lay down on the grave. At midnight the father called, "Is that you, Simon?"

"No, he is sick, and it is I, Foolish Ivan."

"You are a good boy, Ivan. I shall reward you for your obedience. Here is another knot of horsehair. If the need should arise, singe it with a fire and immediately a horse will appear." And again the old man disappeared. Ivan fell asleep and stayed until morning. In the morning he woke up and went home.

"What did you see?" his brothers asked.

"What is to see in a graveyard at night?" said Foolish Ivan as he took off his boots and climbed onto the warm pich.

In the evening they told him to go to the graveyard, because it was his turn. Foolish Ivan put on his boots and went merrily on his way. He lay on the grave and rested. At midnight the father called, "Who is on guard here tonight? Is it Stefan or is it Simon?"

"Neither, Father," said Foolish Ivan, "it was my turn to come, so here I am."

"Good, good." said the father. "Here is another knot of horsehair. If you should need it, it will be of great help to you. Stay healthy, Ivan! There is no need to come again."

Foolish Ivan went home and the brothers asked him, "Did you see anything?"

"What is to see in a graveyard at night?" said Foolish Ivan as he climbed onto the pich and whistled through his teeth.

Shortly after, the king of their country announced that whoever could jump with a horse to the top of a high pole would win his daughter, the princess, as a bride. He had a high pole built with a platform on top where the princess would sit and wait for her husband.

Many young princes and noblemen came from all around, but most of them died or were badly injured trying to jump so high. Their horses tried but did not succeed, and were smashed against the ground.

Still the king said that whoever could jump that high, be it a lord, a peasant or a shoemaker, the princess would be his prize. The brothers heard of this and thought that it was time for them to win the princess. "Let us go! Maybe we will be able to jump that high."

Foolish Ivan said, "Take me along."

"And why do we need you, Foolish Ivan?" they said. "You should just stay home."

"If you do not want to take me, God be with you!" said Foolish Ivan.

As soon as Stefan and Simon rode off, Ivan went into the forest and singed the horsehair with a fire. A snow-white horse appeared, and Ivan climbed into the left ear of the horse and out the right. He instantly became a handsome lad and the clothing on him was like that of a great lord.

Ivan got on the horse and rode off. He caught up to his brothers, whipped them each five times and flew on like a whirlwind. At the palace grounds a large group had gathered and were jumping their horses.

Ivan and his horse jumped most of the way up, but not all the way. They jumped three times and then departed in a cloud of dust.

Ivan returned home, let his horse out into the spring wheat and climbed back onto the warm pich. When his brothers returned he asked them, "What did you find there?"

They replied, "Of all the people there, only one almost jumped high enough. The horse was more beautiful than has been seen before. The rider came flying along the road and whipped us five times, but we do not know why."

"That was me," said Foolish Ivan.

The brothers just laughed. "How could you do such a thing? You do not even have a horse!"

Foolish Ivan lay on the warm pich and smiled to himself behind the chimney.

The next week, they again prepared to go and see the princess.

"Take me with you," said Foolish Ivan.

"Why should you go, Foolish Ivan? Do you think you are needed there?"

"Then I shall sit here on the warm pich."

The brothers rode off, and Foolish Ivan singed the second knot of horsehair with a fire and there appeared before him a bay horse with hair like gold. Ivan climbed into the left ear and came out the right one and became so handsome that there was no one like him on this world.

Ivan mounted the horse, caught up to his brothers, whipped them each five times and then rode on to the palace. When his turn came, Ivan and his horse jumped high enough to brush the platform, but they did not reach the top.

Ivan wheeled around and disappeared down the road. He returned home, released the horse, changed back into his rags and climbed onto the pich. When the brothers returned home, Foolish Ivan asked them, "What did you see?"

"There was such a handsome lad there! But the horse he rode was even better!"

"Oh, you are stupid," said Foolish Ivan. "That was me on that horse."

The brothers laughed and laughed. "Where would you get a horse like that? To sit on the pich, that is for you!"

The third week, they again got ready to go and Foolish Ivan said, "Take me!"

"How can you go? There are some in this world who cannot do anything but sit on a pich."

They left and Foolish Ivan went to the forest and singed the third knot of horsehair, and a beautiful brown horse appeared. He climbed into the left ear and came out the right one, and became so handsome that he could not be described in words. The clothing he wore was made of spun gold.

Ivan mounted the horse and flew like an arrow. He caught up to his brothers, whipped them each five times and rode on. When his turn came, Ivan and the horse jumped right up and landed on the platform beside the princess.

Ivan dismounted and kissed the hand of the princess. She gave him a ring from her finger and tore a silk kerchief in half.

Ivan took the ring and one half of the kerchief, mounted his horse and jumped into the

crowd and disappeared, even though they tried from all sides to catch him.

Ivan rode home, released the horse and climbed onto the warm pich. The brothers returned and he asked them, "What did you see today?"

"Oh, go talk to yourself!" the brothers said. "A horseman rode in, jumped to the top and took a ring and half a kerchief. They wanted to catch him but he fled. We are angry because for the third time he whipped us so soundly that our skin is falling off!"

"That was me," said Foolish Ivan.

The brothers did not even laugh this time, but slouched off to bed. Foolish Ivan put on the ring and sat on the warm pich and smiled to himself. Night fell, but the ring shone so brightly that it woke the brothers.

They came to Foolish Ivan and demanded, "Where did you get that ring?"

"I told you. The princess gave it to me."

"So you really were the one who gave us such a licking with that whip?"

"Of course, I did it! You did not take me with you, and I was getting even with you."

Meanwhile, the princess was sad that she had given away her ring and did not even know to whom. She had fallen completely in love with the handsome lad, and begged her father to find him so that she could marry him.

The king sent soldiers throughout the kingdom, and they eventually came to the house where Foolish Ivan lived. They found him with the ring and dragged him off the pich. Ivan singed one knot of the horsehair and the brown horse appeared. Ivan mounted the horse and rode with the soldiers to the princess. She was happy to see him, and married him and they lived at the palace.

The unsuccessful jumpers who wanted to marry her, however, declared war on her father for allowing a peasant to marry his daughter.

They said that it was not right for her to marry a common peasant and not one of them. The king prepared for battle, and he told Ivan to get ready as well.

Ivan told the king that he was sick, and he did not ride with the king and his army, although his wife went. The battle soon began. Ivan singed the first knot of horsehair and immediately the first beautiful horse appeared. Ivan climbed into the left ear and out the right, and instantly became strong and clad with beautiful armor.

Ivan mounted the horse and rode off to battle. Arriving, he saw that his father-in-law was not doing so well, as there were many enemy soldiers and knights. Ivan drew his sword and attacked the enemy, chopping at the entire army until they turned and fled.

The king wanted to thank him for saving them, but Ivan rode quickly away. He went home, released the horse and lay down to sleep. When the king arrived home, he woke Ivan and told him about the wonderful knight who killed so many warriors and saved them.

Ivan said, "That was me."

"How can that be?" the king said. "You are lazy and good for nothing, but that was a great knight on that beautiful horse!"

A short while later, the enemy again gathered to fight. Once more the king with his army set out to do battle. They told Ivan to go with them, but he said, "You can do without me!"

The king and his army rode off while Ivan lay down to sleep. He slept well, and then went outside and singed the second knot of hair. His horse appeared and he climbed into the left ear and out the right. He became stronger than he was before, sat on his horse and rode off.

Ivan arrived as the battle raged. He threw himself at the enemy, slaying and scattering his foe until they fled. Then he rode home, released the horse and lay down to sleep. The king returned from the battle and said to his daughter, "We struggle for our lives while your beautiful husband lies on his side sleeping!"

She said nothing, but was sad that she had brought such trouble onto her father.

The enemies of the king, after some time, found a witch to help them. She told them that no one could kill the king except for a knight who had been buried for five hundred years beneath the ground. She told them where to find the knight, and they dug him up from his grave. When they explained what they wanted, he said, "Good! Feed my horse for half a year with oats and me with honey, and I will be ready to do your bidding."

The enemies of the king fed them both like boars for the slaughter and in half a year sent notice to the king to do battle again.

The worried king sent messengers to his friends asking that they help him. They came and joined the king and his army.

The king again asked Ivan to go. But he said, "No, I will stay here."

They rode off and Ivan singed the third knot of hair. A horse appeared, the likes of which no one had ever seen. The horse said to Ivan, "Listen! What has gone before is done. Now with the enemy is such a knight that you will have trouble with him. When you fight with him, drive at him from the right side and quickly cut off his head. When you cut it off, jump to the left and you will escape with only a wound in the leg. Climb on, as there is no time to talk!"

Ivan climbed into the left ear and out the right. He became stronger than he was before, sat on his horse and rode off, and the horse carried him like a bird.

Arriving at the battle, he heard a cry for someone to fight with an extraordinary knight. Ivan rode forth against the knight who said, "Greetings, Prince Ivan!"

"And a good day to you, Sir Knight."

The knight then asked, "Are we to fight or to make peace?"

Ivan replied, "I have come here to do battle with you."

"Then let us begin!" said the knight.

They drew their swords and drove together. The first time, they rode past each other. The second time they met, they clashed swords. The third time they met, Ivan and his horse jumped to the right side and Ivan quickly cut off the head of the knight and jumped to the left.

The knight, even without a head, swung his sword and hit Ivan in the leg. His wife ran to him, not recognizing him, and gave him a kerchief to tie up the wound. He tied up his leg and rode away. The enemy, seeing that they could not beat the king and his knight, fled with their army.

The king and the princess returned home with their victorious army. They were pleased that the battle had ended thus, but they would have liked to thank the valiant knight who had won the battle for them.

The princess came to tell Ivan of their victory and found him asleep in their rooms. She saw the wound on his leg bound up with her kerchief and realized who their valiant knight really was.

She called the king and showed him the wound on Ivan. The king woke Ivan and the doctors healed his wound, and they all lived peacefully together in the palace. No one ever dared to attack them again.

An Old Man and a Stone

While walking down the road, an old man stubbed his toe against a stone.

"Why are there such nasty things in this world? Stones like that only litter the road and hurt our feet."

Just then, a fierce black dog came running at him from a nearby yard. The old man cried out in panic, and then picked up the stone and threw it at the dog, who ran away.

"Forgive me for complaining, Lord," said the old man. "I see now that all the things You made, even the smallest ones, have their place in this world."

❖

Over the Fence

A gypsy clambered over a high fence into a garden. As he was deciding what he should take to eat, the lord of the manor burst out of his house.

"You scoundrel! You thief!" he cried. "I shall have you dealt with most severely!"

"Oh, good sir," replied the gypsy, "I do not blame you for being angry. I know you have the right to punish me as you see fit. But I beg of you, please, please do not throw me over the fence."

The lord knew that gypsies are superstitious people, and he decided to do what the gypsy most feared. Accordingly, he grabbed the gypsy by the seat of his pants and the scruff of his neck and heaved him bodily over the fence.

"That ought to take care of him," thought the lord, dusting off his hands.

"May the light of heaven shine upon you forever," called the gypsy. "Now I do not have to go to all the trouble of climbing your high fence. Thank you and goodbye!"

The Ox, the Ram
and the Rooster

Once there was an Ox who was big and strong and proud. His master kept him in a green meadow in summer, but did not feed him very well in winter. Also, the Ox had to work very hard for the master in all seasons. One day the Ox decided that he had had enough of working for someone else, and he ran away.

At first there was plenty of grass to eat, but when autumn came, the grass turned brown. At night the Ox shivered with the cold. A swallow had told him that the birds went to warmer climates for the winter, and the Ox decided to do the same.

The Ox was sorry to leave the beautiful valley where he had been grazing, but there was nothing to be done about it. He set out upon the road where he met a Ram.

"Where are you going?" asked the Ram.

"I am going to a warmer place for the winter," replied the Ox.

"May I go with you?" asked the Ram.

"So be it," replied the Ox.

The two went on down the road and soon met up with a Rooster.

"And where are you off to on this fine day?" asked the Rooster.

"We are going to a warmer place to spend the winter," they said.

"I would like to join you," said the Rooster.

Now there were three travelling together. They walked and walked and, when evening came, they stopped in a meadow to rest. As they were resting, they heard a great clamor of geese honking overhead.

"Geese!" cried the Rooster. "Let us go with them; they know where to go."

The Rooster tried to follow the Geese, but his wings were not strong enough and he barely got off the ground. Although he flapped and crowed, he could not get into the air. He came back to the others and grumbled about his luck.

"All that effort," he said, "and all I got for my trouble was tired."

The Geese, meanwhile, had landed nearby and an old Gander came up to the three friends and greeted them with a bow.

"May I ask what you three are doing in a spot like this?" said the Gander.

"We are travelling to a warm place to spend the winter," said the Ox.

"You will not get there," said the Gander.

"What do you mean?" asked the Rooster.

"The Lord made you for other things," replied the Gander. "With legs like the Ox and Ram have and wings like you have, it would take you a lifetime to reach a warmer climate."

The Gander returned to his flock and left the three friends discussing his words. The Ox, the Ram and the Rooster tried to think what they should do, but were able to come up with no plan. They finally agreed to go to the old Gander and ask him what to do.

"I suggest you return to the places where you came from," said the Gander. "You will experience nothing but hardship on the road, and perhaps your masters will take you back if you ask their forgiveness."

The three friends thought about the words of the Gander.

"The Gander is a wise old bird," they said, "but we did not go to all this trouble just to return to the hardship of our earlier lives."

The Ox, the Ram and the Rooster went into the nearby forest where they built themselves a little house, and they are living there to this very day, without a care in the world.

The Sheep and the Fox

Once there was a flock of sheep that grazed in a meadow. A fox lived nearby, and she was always bothering the sheep, trying to run off with the young lambs or the weaker sheep.

One sheep was getting on in age. She was too old to keep up with the flock, and was always being left behind.

The fox decided that this sheep would be next on her menu. The problem was that the fox was also getting old; it was not easy for her to hunt as she used to when she was younger.

"Since I am not as strong or as agile as I used to be," she thought, "I will have to use my cunning to get the sheep into a place where she cannot escape. Sheep are stupid, anyway, and I should have no trouble tricking her."

The fox began to spend time around the old sheep. "The other sheep do not respect you, because you are old," she told the sheep. "I am also getting old, but everybody still needs companionship. You could come and live with me on the other side of the hedge. There is much nicer grass there."

The old sheep listened to the honeyed words of the fox and decided that she would go and at least see what the fox was offering her.

"Very well," said the sheep. "Let us go and see what is on the other side of the hedge."

As they walked, the fox kept feeling the sheep to see how much meat there was on her bones. She felt her ribs and squeezed her legs, which made the sheep nervous.

"Things may not be as they seem," thought the sheep. "I do not trust this fox."

When they got to the hole in the hedge, the fox said, "After you, my dear friend. I will be right behind you."

The sheep was afraid of the fox by this time and she said, "This hole is too small for me to go through. Let us go to a bigger hole farther down the hedge." The sheep led the fox to a hole where she had seen the master set a fox trap that morning. She said, "Here is a bigger hole, dear fox. Go through first and see if it is safe for me to follow you."

The fox quickly ducked into the hole and was trapped, and the happy sheep ran off to rejoin her flock.

The Soldier and Death

A soldier served the Tsar for thirty-three years and then was released. The Tsar gave him three copper coins and sent him on his way. This is how the Tsar thanked his faithful soldiers. The soldier walked and walked until he came across three beggars.

"Alms for the poor, Master," they said.

The soldier gave one coin to the beggars.

In a while he met three more beggars.

"Alms for the poor, Master," they said.

The soldier brought out a second coin and gave it to the beggars.

Later he came across three more beggars.

"Alms for the poor, Master," they said.

The soldier brought out his last coin and gave it to the beggars.

He went on and thought, "What will happen now that I have given away my three coins?" Coming down the road toward him, he saw three more beggars.

"Alms for the poor, Master," they said.

The soldier gave them his coat.

"With what shall we reward you for giving us alms?" said the beggars.

"The soldier replied, "I would like to have a magic bag. When I think of money, let the bag be full. When I need food, let the bag supply it. When I need anything done, let the bag do it for me. Whatever I think of, let it immediately be."

"It shall be, good servant. Go with God."

The three beggars said this and disappeared, as if they had not been there, and the soldier walked on.

The soldier thought to himself, "Let us see if they did not lie."

He stuffed his hand into his pocket and pulled out a bag, which was full of money.

He sat down to rest, looked at the bag and thought of food. Instantly, it was before him.

"Eh," he said, "this is good." He ate his fill and drank well, and then the bag cleaned everything up. He looked up and saw a pair of ducks flying. He opened the bag and said, "Into the bag!" Instantly, the ducks flew into it.

The soldier eventually walked into a city where lived a rich merchant with a huge house that was not lived in because devils occupied it.

The soldier found the merchant and asked him, "What will you give me if I drive the devils out of your house?"

"If you can drive them out," he said, "I will take care of you for life."

The merchant fed the soldier and he went to spend the night in the house. At midnight he heard a great knocking and thundering. The floor cracked open and a devil crawled out.

"What do you want?" asked the soldier.

"I will eat you!" cried the devil.

The soldier opened the bag and said, "Into the bag!" Screaming, the devil flew into the bag. The soldier tied the bag and beat it with a stick.

"Let me out! I will stop my people from coming to this house," cried the devil.

The soldier let him out and the devil ran back through the hole in the floor.

In the morning the soldier led the merchant into the house and told him that the devils had all gone. The merchant was pleased, and he gave orders for his family to be moved into the house, along with the soldier.

The soldier and the merchant lived well and in peace for many years.

Finally, it came time for the soldier to die and he ordered, "Place this little bag in the coffin with me, without fail."

This was done, and he was buried. He arrived at the other world, and saw that he was in Hell. Immediately he knocked a peg into the wall and hung his rifle there.

"Is there whisky here?" he asked.

"There is."

"Is there tobacco?"

"There is.

"Fire?"

"There is."

"Then this is not Hell," said the soldier. "This is Heaven, such Heaven!"

The soldier marched through Hell, ordering people about, like an officer.

Eventually he came upon the same devil he had beat in the world above. When the devil saw the soldier he cried, "This is the one who once beat me badly! He will never give us any peace. We must be rid of him somehow."

The devils became afraid. They ran away from Hell and locked the soldier inside.

Once safely outside, the devils planned to be rid of the soldier. "Let us cast lots, brothers. On whoever it falls, we will stretch him over a barrel like a drum. Then we will strike the drum and maybe the soldier will leave."

They cast lots, stretched a devil over a barrel, and beat him like a drum.

The soldier heard the drum and cried, "Ah, a war is starting, a military campaign!" He grabbed his rifle and ran out, while the devils jumped in and slammed the door.

The soldier walked upon the earth, thinking that there was no home for him, until St Peter met him one day.

"Go to Heaven," said St Peter. "They have been waiting for you for a long time."

The soldier went to Heaven and God placed him as a guard by the palace. He stood guard and saw Death approaching. The soldier asked her, "Where are you going?"

"To God, servant."

"For what?"

"To ask what to do on earth."

"Wait here; I will go ask."

The soldier went to God, saying, "Death has come, asking what she is to do on earth."

God replied, "Let her take only the old people for three years."

Returning to Death, the soldier remembered his brothers. "Death will take them," he thought.

He said to Death, "God has ordered that you gnaw on old oak trees for three years."

After three years Death again came to God. The soldier asked, "Where are you going?"

"To God, servant."

"For what?"

"To ask what to do on earth."

"Wait here; I will go ask."

The soldier went to God, saying, "Death has come, asking what she is to do on earth."

"Tell her to take middle-aged people."

The soldier thought, "But I may have relatives among them."

He came outside and said: "God said to gnaw on middle-aged oaks for three years."

"Thank you, servant," said Death.

Three years later Death again appeared, and she was very thin.

"Servant, ask God what I am to do."

The soldier went to God, saying, "Death has come, asking what she is to do on earth."

"Let her take small children," said God.

Remembering that he had grandchildren, the soldier said to Death, "God said that you must gnaw on young oaks for three years."

Death thanked him and left. Three more years passed and this time, the soldier did not see Death approaching, and she sneaked in to see God. She complained to God that He was punishing her with hunger.

"The soldier lied to you!" said God. "Go and take him right now."

Death said to the soldier, "You must give me your soul!"

But the soldier opened his little bag and said, "Into the bag!"

Death immediately jumped into the bag. The soldier quickly tied up the bag and threw it into the mud.

The Wonderful Plant

When the world was young and there were not many people on this world, everybody was properly thankful for their existence. God was happy with this, as the people respected Him and the world He had created.

God was so pleased with the people that He decided to create a special plant for them. He would create a plant that would be good for medicine, food, cloth, and anything else that was needed, even for making beer.

God created the wonderful plant and spread it all over the world. In the spring, the people found the plant and discovered its many uses. And they were properly thankful to God for the bounty He had so graciously bestowed on them.

The plant was not only useful, but beautiful to look at and smell, and the little soft hairs on its leaves made it a pleasure to handle. The people used it for almost everything. They cured their aches with it, stopped bleeding from wounds, washed their hair with its water, brewed beer from it and completely enjoyed it.

After a time, however, the people became used to the plant, and they started to take it for granted. Whenever they needed some of the plant, they began to rip up and discard the plants that were not perfect. They trampled on the plant, and no longer respected it.

God looked down and saw how the people no longer respected His gift, and He was sorely disappointed. "If they no longer respect the plant I have given them, they shall no longer have it," God said. And He caused the plant to vanish from the earth.

The people missed the wonderful plant, and they realized that God was punishing them for not acting properly. They fell on their knees and prayed to God for the return of the plant.

God heard their prayers and relented. But He changed the plant to ensure that the people would appreciate His gift. The plant became what we know today as the stinging nettle. It is a very useful plant, but if you do not handle it with respect, you will suffer for it.

Notes on the Tales

Page 11   Cossack Mamaryha

The retelling of this story is adapted from versions found in several collections in both Ukrainian and English. The word "Cossack" is often spelled "Kozak," but since "Cossack" has entered the English language with that spelling, I am using it rather than "Kozak."

Page 29   The Devil at the Wedding

This story comes from Mary Shewchuk of Vegreville, Alberta. Once again, it is a good thing that people like Mary record their stories so that the rest of us can share in them.

Page 33   The Devil Serpent

Found in a few collections, this tale is typical of those stories that have been told and retold so often that they have changed character, depending on the storyteller. Under the Communist régime, many Ukrainian folk tales were retold with a very Soviet or Russian bias, and I have attempted to restore the Ukrainian flavor to such stories, but that is not easy to do.

Page 63   The Falcon Hunter and the King

Rena Patrick of Heriot Bay, BC told me this one. Her great-grandmother, Baba Kalbida from Saskatchewan, told the story, and we can all be happy that Rena remembered it. I just love the little twist to the ending of the story.

Page 69   Feet on the Pillow

Sandra Fedoruk of Saskatoon, Saskatchewan spent her growing-up years close to her baba Maria Yakimchuk, and she heard many, many stories, most of which she still remembers. Some of the stories are true, others are sad, and still others are just for fun, like this one.

Usually, there is something to be learned from the stories Baba and Dido used to tell the children. It is still a wonderful way to share knowledge with the young people of our world.

Page 73   Garlic

Robert Larionyk told me this story. It is similar to the current joke in which a man takes a bag of gold bricks to Heaven and St Peter asks him why he would bring paving blocks to Heaven. We learn from such stories that the value of anything depends on who is looking at it.

Page 81   Gossip

Myrtle Anderson told me about this story several years ago. She remembered it from a reader she used while she was teaching in the schools of Saskatchewan. I searched without success for the story in all the old readers I could find, and then Sandra Fedoruk, out of the blue, told me the story! Thanks again go to everyone who shares their stories with us.

Page 85   How Foolish Ivan Married
the Princess

There are many stories about fools or dummies who wind up as heroes. They help to make us feel better about ourselves, since, if even Foolish Ivan could marry a princess, we might be able to do better with our own lives.

This story is like many others of its kind; it starts in one area, the death of the father and the obligations of the sons to stand guard at the grave, then goes off into a completely different scene full of magic and strange things, all of which our hero accepts without a thought. The world is just going on as it should, as far as Ivan is concerned.

Page 103   An Old Man and a Stone

This story is from JB Rudnyckyj's book 'Ukrainian-Canadian Folklore in English Translation.' Professor Rudnyckyj collected many stories at a time when many pioneers were still alive and well. It is a good thing he did.

Page 104   Over the Fence

Sandra Fedoruk told me this story, along with many others. It is quite similar to the Brer Rabbit stories of Joel Chandler Harris, as well as many other trickster tales found in every culture. Tricksters teach us the value of quick thought while they entertain us with their antics.

Page 107   The Ox, the Ram and the Rooster

This is a typical animal story that could be found in many cultures. Here we learn that we should accept what we are and not try to become something we are not meant to be.

Page 113   The Sheep and the Fox

This is another of Mary Shewchuk's wonderful stories. While the Fox is often portrayed as the smart one or the trickster, here she is the one who is fooled. Not to underestimate others is a message we find often in such stories.

Page 117   The Soldier and Death

This is another of the stories found in several collections. This particular retelling is based on a translation by J Zurowsky of Winnipeg, Manitoba. Mr Zurowsky also translated "Kharkiv," which was published by Ethnic Enterprises in 1996. I am indeed pleased to have Mr Zurowsky's translations of many of the stories that appear in these books.

Page 127   The Wonderful Plant

Rena Patrick heard this story from Steve, who she met while picking nettles one day. I would like to find Steve, as he likely knows more stories. Unfortunately, Rena never learned his last name or anything else about him. We can only hope that he continues to share his stories with the people he meets along the way.

   —Danny Evanishen, Publisher

In this glossary:

[a] is pronounced as in far
[e] is pronounced as in get
[ee] is pronounced as in feet
[i] is pronounced as in sit
[o] is pronounced as between got and goat
[oo] is pronounced as in loose
[y] is pronounced as in yes

[kh] is pronounced as in Scottish loch
[zh] is pronounced as in vision